MOM *and* ME

Introduction

Moms teach.

Moms play.

Moms are beautiful.

Meet three children and their moms.

Written and photographed by John Kaplan

SCHOLASTIC INC. Cartwheel ·B·O·O·K·S·®

New York Toronto London Auckland Sydney

To my own mom, Ruth Kaplan, whose creativity and zest for life
will always be inspiring. I love you, Mom.

Acknowledgments

Thank you to all of the people who have opened their lives to me and generously offered their time, advice, and friendship. To the families and some great moms: Donald, Marlene, Donald Sr., Deirdre, Deanna, and Dominique Davis; Kate, Linda, and Anthony Gomulka; Jonathan, Joyce, Brian, and Sara Scott; Adrienne and Kathleen Cannella; Nicky and Michelle Cifrulak; Melissa and Dana Newman-Evans; Daniel, Lynn, and Paul Ren; and Stephen and Jacqueline Tauriello. To all of the teachers and fine Pittsburgh area schools: Bud Alder and the Keystone Oaks School District; Gregg Beyer and Aiken Elementary; Mr. Valicenti and the Montour School District; Larry Snyder and Jefferson Elementary; and Marianna Gaffney, Susan Stauber, and Sheryl Zeppenfeld at Burkett Elementary. My own family and "feels like" family: My hero, Dad Ralph Kaplan, Grandma Margaret Denkin, Jenny and Jim Griffin, Laurie Jones and Camille, Sally Kaplan, and the memory of Grandpa Max, Grandma Anne, Spot, Dot, Keesh, and some cool cats: Wild Fire, Inca, Wally, et al. To my good friends at the JR: Pat Coburn, Bill Hagen, Barry Locher, Greg Mellis, Dave and Judy Spencer family, and all the photogs. To John Durniak and *The New York Times*; Bill Pekala and Nikon Inc.; and Ann Hughes, Rich Henry and Kennywood, the coaster capital of the world. To Scholastic art director Edie Weinberg, Tara Doyle, Kimberly Shapiro, Amy Canning, and especially to my editor, Grace Maccarone, for guidance and good advice!

Library of Congress Cataloging-in-Publication Data

Kaplan, John, 1959-
 Mom and me/by John Kaplan.
  p. cm.
 ISBN 0-590-47294-1
 1. Mother and child — Juvenile literature. 2. Mothers — Juvenile literature. I. Title
HQ755.85.K365 1996   95-19499
306.874'3—dc20   CIP
                                                                AC

12 11 10 9 8 7 6 5 4 3 2 1   6 7 8 9/9 0 1/0

CVRU
HQ
755.85
.K365
1996

Printed in Singapore   46
First Scholastic printing, March 1996

MOM *and* KATE

We'll Be Best Friends Forever

My name is Kate.
I love Mom and
she loves me.

We shop together in the supermarket.

We cook.

We play games.

Sometimes I make Mom stay in the playhouse. She can't come out until I say so!

We work together in the garden.

We relax and watch our favorite videos, too.

I like to surprise her. For Mother's Day, Dad and I gave Mom
a super surprise — breakfast in bed!

When I grow up,
I want to be just
like her.

We'll be best
friends forever.

MOM *and* JONATHAN

Sometimes Mom Acts Like a Kid

My name is Jonathan. My mom likes to play almost as much as I do.

Mom says, "You're never too old to ride the roller coaster."

But she's way too big to ride the seesaw with me!

Saturday is cleanup day at our house. Since Dad doesn't live at home, I work extra hard to help out.

Saturday sure is a "Smelly Day"!

After we're done
with the house,
it's Mom's turn
to clean me.
Baths are fun, but I
don't like haircuts.

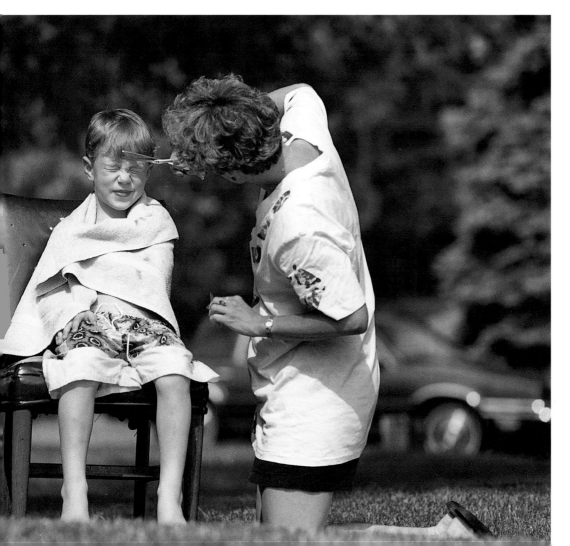

I have a brother
named Brian,
a sister named Sara,
and a cat called Sunny.
Together, we're a family.

Sometimes we paint the house…

...and sometimes we paint each other!

I love baseball.
Mom comes to every game.
She cheers for me when I'm safe…

…and even when I'm out.

Win or lose,
I say, "Hey, Mom!
Slap me five!"

MOM *and* DONALD

Mom Knows How to Make Me Laugh

My name is Donald and I am six years old.

Mom knows how to make me laugh.

She says that now I'm old enough to remember to clean my room.

I like helping Mom
with baby Dominique.

We go to the park with my sisters, Deirdre and Deanna. But sometimes I like to have Mom all to myself.

I'm teaching her
how to play soccer.
She's getting better,
but I'm still the best!

I think she's the most
beautiful mom in the world.
She listens when I have
something important to say.

I need her when I'm sad.

Best of all, she knows what makes me happy. And Mom says I make her happy, too.